Noisy Bird

Sing-Along

DAWN PUBLICATIONS

By John Himmelman

For Ed Ricciuti

Library of Congress Cataloging-in-Publication Data

Himmelman, John, author, illustrator.
  Noisy bird sing-along / by John Himmelman. -- First edition.
    pages cm
  Summary: "Listen to the birds! They are often very noisy. You can tell what kind of bird it is just by listening. It's fun to learn their sounds and to sing along"-- Provided by the publisher.
  Audience: Ages 4-9.
  Audience: K to grade 3.
  ISBN 978-1-58469-513-4 (hardback) -- ISBN 978-1-58469-514-1 (pbk.) 1. Birdsongs--Juvenile literature. 2. Birds--Behavior--Juvenile literature. 3. Birds--Identification--Juvenile literature. I. Title.

  QL698.5.H56 2015
  598.159'4--dc23

                              2014031421

Book design and production by Patty Arnold, *Menagerie Design & Publishing*

Manufactured by Regent Publishing Services, Hong Kong
Printed December, 2014, in ShenZhen, Guangdong, China

10 9 8 7 6 5 4 3 2 1
First Edition

Dawn Publications
12402 Bitney Springs Road
Nevada City, CA 95959
530-274-7775
nature@dawnpub.com

We love to listen to the singing birds! Each one has its very own song. Let's sing those songs with them.

Some bird songs sound like sentences.

A **Robin** starts the morning with a cheerful wish.

CHEERY UP?

CHEERIO!

CHEERY UP? CHEERIO!

A wet lawn is a favorite place for Robins to hunt for worms.

White-throated Sparrows add a warm tune to a cold winter morning.

Oh Sweet Canada

Canada Canada

Sparrows look for seeds and berries in the thick bushes.

A Yellow Warbler sings sweetly near a stream.

Sweet Sweet I'm so

Sweet!

Yellow Warblers nest in wetlands, where there are plenty of insects to eat.

The deep voice of a **Barred Owl** seems to ask a question.

Who

cooks
for you?

Who cooks

for you allll?

Most owls hunt for small mammals at night,
when the mammals are most active.

Some birds say their name!
A Black-capped Chickadee pops up
on a branch.

Chick-a dee-dee-dee

Chick-a-dee-dee-dee

Black-capped Chickadees live in woodlands where they find plenty of insects and seeds to eat.

A Whip-poor-will whistles

WHIP-PO

WHIP-PO

A Whip-poor-will's wide mouth helps it
gulp up insects while it's flying.

from the edge of a swamp.

OR-WILL

OR-WILL

Some birds just make sounds.
A Mallard quacks in a pond.

QUACK
QUACK
QUACK

QUACK QUACK
ck
ck
QUACK

Mallards are "dabbling ducks." They tip their bodies forward underwater to find seeds and water plants.

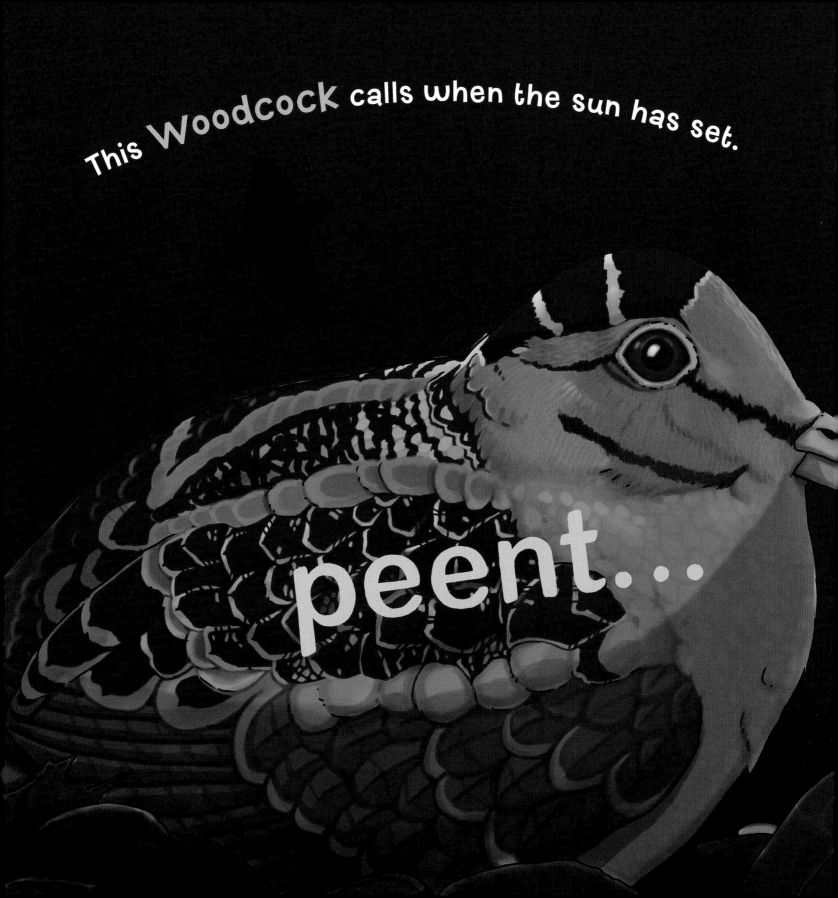

This Woodcock calls when the sun has set.

peent...

peent...   peent...

peent...

Woodcocks' eyes are near the top of the head so they can look for danger from above while poking for worms in the soil.

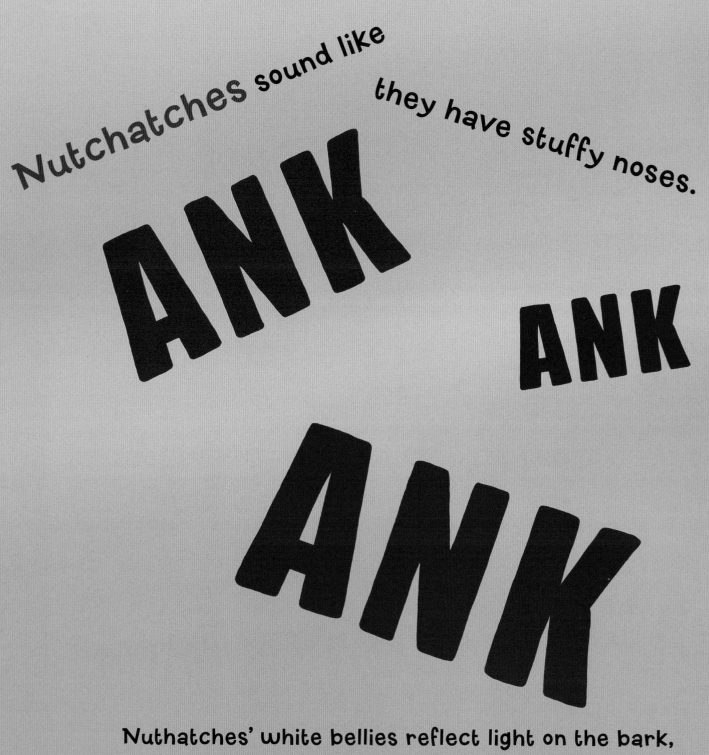

Nutchatches sound like they have stuffy noses.

ANK ANK ANK

Nuthatches' white bellies reflect light on the bark, which helps them find insects.

Hummingbird wings hum in a blur of motion!

hmmmmmm

Hummingbirds zip from flower to flower to sip sweet nectar.

A **House Sparrow** chirps from atop a brick wall.

Many House Sparrows live in crowded cities where they search for crumbs in parking lots.

A Downy Woodpecker taps away on a hollow branch.

tap

ap

tap

tap

tap

tap

tap

Downy Woodpeckers tap into
trees and bark to find beetle
larvae, caterpillars, and
other insects to eat.

p

Who cooks
for you?

Chick-a-
dee-dee-dee

Who cooks
for you alllll?

CHEERY UP?

Oh
Sweet
Canada

Canada
Canada

CHEERIO!

K

CHEERP CHEERP

mmmmmmmmmmmmmmmm

Fun Facts About the Birds

Birds make all kinds of sounds. Sometimes males sing songs to attract females. Other times they sing to keep other males out of the area. Females and males make sounds so they know where each other is while they are looking for food. Many birds make noises to scare off predators.

When **American Robins** hunt for food, they tip their head sideways. Are they listening for worms? No! One eye looks up for hawks. The other looks down for worms. One robin may eat 14 feet of earthworms a day.

Most birds sing in spring. But **White-throated Sparrows** also sing in winter. Look for the patch of white on the chin.

Yellow Warblers are small songbirds. They weigh less than a quarter. Sometimes they even get caught in an orb spider's web.

Barred Owls are nicknamed "Monkey Owls" because they make loud, monkey-like calls. They swallow small mammals whole. Then they cough up the bones and fur in a hard pellet. You can find the pellets at the bottom of a tree where they roost.

Black-capped Chickadees stash seeds to eat later. Each chickadee can remember thousands of hiding places. They like to come to bird feeders. You can even train them to take seeds from your hand!

Eastern Whip-poor-wills call at night. They can be hard to see. But in the beam of a flashlight you can see their eyes glow like fire. They hunt flying insects at dawn and dusk, catching them with their big, wide mouths.

You can find **Mallards** paddling in lakes, rivers, puddles, and ponds. Look for the male's bright green head. And listen for the female's loud quack. The males make a quieter call.

Male **American Woodcocks** show off for females by doing a sky dance. In the spring they circle high in the air. The wind in their feathers makes a twittering sound. They end their dance with a steep dive to the ground.

White-breasted Nuthatches run up and down the sides of trees. Pinch your nose shut when you sing along with them in this book. You'll sound more like them!

Anna's Hummingbirds beat their wings 30-50 times per second. Hang a feeder filled with sugar water outside your window to get a close look.

House Sparrows have lived near people for hundreds of years. You'll see them wherever there are buildings. But you won't find them in natural places like forests.

Downy Woodpeckers are little birds that make a big sound. When they tap on hollow trees it's called drumming. The loud noise attracts females and warns other males to stay away.

Birdy Things to Do

Pishing

Birds are curious creatures. If there is trouble in the area, they want to know about it. Many birds give an alarm call to warn the flock of predators. Chickadees and titmice give a warning that sounds like "Pssh Pssh Pssh." When other perching birds hear this, they pop out into the open to see what's going on.

By imitating this sound, you can get hidden birds to show themselves. Stay perfectly still, and go, "Pssh pssh pssh" in an area where there are birds. You can often get the same results by making squeaky kissing noises on the back of your hand.

Once you see the birds, stop making the sound. It's important to let them get back to what they were doing before you interrupted them.

Feeding

Photograph by Bill Kobak

One of the best ways to find birds is to bring them to you. Humans have been feeding birds for centuries. We love to have them visit us. So do our cats, but for a different reason—so please keep your cats inside.

Some birds, like sparrows, blackbirds, and jays will eat corn and other seeds scattered on the ground. Many birds will be attracted to hanging feeders filled with sunflower or thistle seeds. Woodpeckers will come to suet (animal fat) in a small cage attached to a tree. Bluebirds love insects, and a tray filled with mealworms will keep them coming back for more. If you live in a place with no yard, you can get a feeder that attaches to your window with suction cups. You will get hours of entertainment—close up!

Don't forget water! In some areas where it is very hot, or cold, water can be hard to find. A birdbath filled with water will not only quench their thirst, but many will use it as a bath!

Listing

Many people like to keep a list of the birds they see. You can start a list of birds you saw or heard in your yard, town, country, or on your travels. A lot of birders keep a "life list'" which lists all the birds they've seen in their life. Some people even keep a list of the birds in their dreams! When you get to know what bird makes what sound, you can list birds even without seeing them. The fun in doing this is adding new birds to your list. It becomes a never-ending treasure hunt. The longer you watch birds, the more you see. The more you see, the harder it is to find one you've never seen before. But when you do find a new one, it makes it even more special.

Birding

Birding was once called "bird watching." People who set out to find birds are called "birders." A field guide and a pair of binoculars help you identify birds unfamiliar to you. One thing that makes birding especially fun is doing it with other people. Every state and province has several organizations that schedule trips to find birds. It is the best way to learn about what you are seeing.

There are also games birders play. One is called a "Big Day," in which you try to find as many birds as you can in 24 hours. The "Big Sit!" is an annual event where you sit in one place for 24 hours and count how many birds you see and hear from a 17-foot circle. There are too many events to list here, but you can learn about them from a local nature center, bird club, or Audubon club.

Resources

Audubon Adventures — An environmental education program featuring high-interest classroom materials and engaging website about birds, wildlife, and their habitats. Materials and activities are correlated to Common Core and National Science standards. www.audubonadventures.org/

Feeder Watch Project — A citizen science project that engages children in the excitement of nature study and the wonder of scientific investigation. Teachers and parents get everything they need to identify, count, and report bird observation. http://feederwatch.org/

Bird Sleuth K-12 — Kits, free resources, and other hands-on materials for teachers and home school parents. Resources may be used as a full curriculum or stand-alone activities. Observing birds at least once a week can enhance students' interest in the local habitat and their ability to think scientifically. www.birdsleuth.org/

JOHN HIMMELMAN has traveled the world in search of birds. He is a past president of the New Haven Bird Club in Connecticut and leads birding trips for various organizations. He also created "The Big Sit!"—an event in which participants all over the planet choose one spot, a 17-foot circle, to count all the birds they see and hear in 24 hours. John is the author and/or illustrator of over 75 books for children. He is married to Betsy, a high school art teacher. Visit his website at www.johnhimmelman.com for information on his books and programs.

ALSO BY JOHN HIMMELMAN

Noisy Bug Sing-Along — Bugs can be very LOUD! And they have no "voices," but instead rub legs or wings together, or use other body parts to make the sounds. Fascinating! **Available as a book app — each page animated plus an interactive game at the end.**

Noisy Frog Sing-Along — Frogs make all kinds of weird and wonderful sounds—all without ever opening their mouths! Enjoy John's great close-up illustrations and croak! **Available as a book app — each page animated plus an interactive game at the end.**

A FEW OTHER NATURE AWARENESS BOOKS FROM DAWN PUBLICATIONS

In the Trees, Honey Bees — Remarkable inside-the-hive views of bees offer insights into the lives of these important insects.

Near One Cattail: Turtles, Logs and Leaping Frogs — A whole community of creatures live in a bog-boggy place. No child will be able to resist exploring wetlands.

Molly's Organic Farm — Wind blows the gate open, and Molly, a homeless cat, scampers through — and discovers the magical interplay of nature on an organic farm.

Eliza and the Dragonfly — Almost despite herself, Eliza becomes entranced by an "awful" dragonfly nymph — and before long, both of them are transformed. "Magnificent!"

The Prairie That Nature Built — A romp above, below, and all around a beautiful and exciting habitat. Rhythm and rhyme reinforce the richness of dynamic prairie life.

Over in the Ocean and *Over in the Jungle* are two best-selling counting books that introduce the baby animals in these fascinating habitats. Both books are now also available as award-winning apps — animated, interactive games!

Dawn Publications is dedicated to inspiring in children a deeper understanding and appreciation for all life on Earth. You can browse through our titles, download resources for teachers, and order at www.dawnpub.com or call 800-545-7475.